Forever
Champions

Forever Champions

Richard Brignall

James Lorimer & Company, Ltd., Publishers
Toronto

James Lorimer & Company Ltd. acknowledges the support of the Ontario Arts Council. We acknowledge the support of the Government of Canada through the Book Publishing Industry Development Program (BPIDP) for our publishing activities. We acknowledge the support of the Canada Council for the Arts for our publishing program. We acknowledge the assistance of the OMDC Book Fund, an initiative of Ontario Media Development Corporation.

Cover design: Kate Moore and Meghan Collins

Library and Archives Canada Cataloguing in Publication

Brignall, Richard
    Forever champions : the legacy of the Edmonton Grads / Richard Brignall.

(Recordbooks)
ISBN 978-1-55028-977-0 (bound). — ISBN 978-1-55028-976-3 (pbk.)

    1. Edmonton Commercial Graduates (Basketball team) — History — Juvenile literature. 2. McDougall Commercial High School (Edmonton, Alta.) — Sports — History — Juvenile literature. 3. Basketball — Alberta — Edmonton — History — Juvenile literature. I. Title. II. Series.

| GV885.42.E3B75 2007 | j796.323097123'34 | C2007-900360-5 |

James Lorimer & Company Ltd., Publishers
317 Adelaide Street West, Suite #1002
Toronto, ON
M5V 1P9
www.lorimer.ca

Distributed in the United States by:
Orca Book Publishers
P.O. Box 468
Custer, WA USA
98240-0468

Printed and bound in Canada

Contents

I would like to dedicate this book to all the players that wore Edmonton Grads colours. This group of tremendously talented and courageous women are role models for everybody. The Grads played an important role in the advancement of women's sports.
They should not be forgotten.

Prologue

The story of the Edmonton Grads begins with a coin toss.

In 1914, J. Percy Page and Ernest Hyde were teachers at McDougall Commercial High School in Edmonton, Alberta. The school was brand new and did not have anyone to teach physical education to girls. Either Page or Hyde would have to lead the classes.

Back then, a lot of people did not believe that girls could be athletes. They thought girls lacked the strength to play sports. They worried girls could hurt themselves. Some even said that female athletes would not be able to have children. And sports were not ladylike.

Neither man wanted to do it. So, they decided to flip a coin.

Page lost the toss. Never a poor sport, he decided to make the most of it. He would teach the girls a game he knew and loved: basketball.

Page had played the game in his youth and had coached boys' teams in New Brunswick and Ontario. He read many books about developing basketball skills. He knew how to train young players.

To Page's delight, the McDougall Commercial girls learned the game quickly. He formed a team with the best players. They competed against other school teams in Edmonton. In their first year, they won every game. As the city's top schoolgirls' team, they earned the Richardson trophy.

Later that same year, McDougall Commercial High School won the first-ever provincial championship. They were the top team in the province.

Following their big win, many of the teammates graduated high school. To continue playing, they formed a new team.

McDougall School Team 1919–20

The History of Basketball

Did you know that a Canadian invented basketball? Dr. James Naismith was born in Almonte, Ontario. Later, he graduated from McGill University. In 1891, he was the head of athletics at the YMCA Training School in Springfield, Massachusetts. The school gave him a big challenge. In just 14 days, he had to create a new indoor game. There was a gap between football in autumn, and soccer and track in spring. The new game needed to keep students active in winter.

Naismith recalled a childhood game called duck-on-a-rock. Players had to knock a a stone (called a "duck") off a larger rock by tossing a smaller rock at it. This simple idea led to the sport now known as basketball. The training school played the first game with a soccer ball and two peach baskets. It started with 13 rules of play. In 1892, Naismith published the first formal rules of the new game.

Naismith lived to see basketball become one of the world's most popular games. When he died in 1939, it was a sport enjoyed by both men and women.

They called themselves the Commercial Graduates Basketball Club of Edmonton. Before long, most people knew them as simply the Edmonton Grads.

Page stayed on as their manager and coach. The teacher who lost the coin toss would lead his team to greatness.

1 Women Pick up the Ball

American Senda Berenson is known as the mother of women's basketball. She was an athletic teacher at Smith College in Boston, Massachusetts.

Heiress Sophia Smith founded Smith College in 1871. At the time, very few women attended colleges or universities. Smith thought society would be much better off if more women got higher educations. She believed that it had to be equal to the education men were getting at other colleges. Today, Smith College is one of the top schools in the United States.

In 1892 — before any of the Edmonton Grads were even born — Berenson was setting up athletic programs at Smith College. She wanted to create well-rounded women. Athletics were key.

"The aim in athletics for women should above all things be health — physical health and moral health," said Berenson.

To accomplish that, she wanted to include women of all skill levels. Sports, she felt, would build character in her students. Berenson heard about a new game called basketball. She visited the game's inventor, Dr. Naismith, to learn more about it.

Berenson knew she had found a great game for her students. But she worried that the sport was too rough. Like many people at the time, she thought women could get hurt easily. So, she changed the rules to make women's basketball a gentler game.

Under Naismith's rules, players could not run if they had the ball. They had to throw it from the spot where they caught it. An opponent could get the ball by snatching or hitting it out of a player's hands. Berenson didn't want her students fighting over the ball. Snatching and hitting were not allowed in her version of the game.

In men's basketball, any player could go after a ball that was out of bounds. Whoever got to it first could put it back into play. This led to wild races after the ball! Berenson would have none of that.

She divided the court into three equal zones: guard, centre, and forward. Both teams would have an equal number of players on the court (six or nine) and an equal number of players in each zone (either two or three). They could not cross into other zones. Instead, players moved the ball between zones by passing or dribbling. Also, a player was not allowed to hold the ball for more than three seconds. She could only dribble it three times while she was moving. When she dribbled, the ball had to bounce up past her knees. This gave opponents a chance to steal it mid-air.

The first collegiate women's basketball game was played on March 21, 1893, at Smith College. The freshman class played the sophomore class.

The gym doors were locked so that male spectators could not enter. Why were men kept out? Back then, women were supposed to be modest and well mannered. They showed as little of their bodies as possible. They did not let men see them running and sweating. But if men had snuck in, they would not have seen much. The players wore floor-length dresses! The only body parts that weren't covered were their hands, necks, and heads.

A lot of women had a hard time playing in this clothing. They tripped over their skirts, and they often got hurt.

Then bloomers came along. They were loose-fitting pants gathered just above the knee. The pants were worn with stockings underneath. Women could run in bloomers, but they were hot and bulky. The players also wore long-sleeved shirts. At least it was better than wearing dresses.

In time, men were allowed to watch women's basketball. With players wearing lighter uniforms, a lot of men turned up!

Berenson's rules for women's basketball were first published in 1899. Two years later, she became the editor of the first women's basketball guide. The guide spread her version of women's basketball.

In 1985, Berenson was inducted to the Basketball Hall of Fame. She was inducted into the Women's Basketball Hall of Fame in 1999.

Playing by the Rules

Women were told to be very careful when they first started playing basketball. Many people didn't think their bodies could handle a lot of stress. They wanted women to exercise, but not too much. Berenson created rules to keep female players from pushing themselves too hard. Here are a few found in an article by Berenson titled "Basketball at Smith College" from 1914 — the same year the Edmonton Grads started playing.

• No girl may play for four days when she is physically unfit.
• Every student must wear bloomers and gymnasium blouse and jumper and black shoes and stockings.
• No girl may play more than twice a week.
• A girl who plays basketball twice a week may not play field hockey, and vice versa. If a girl plays basketball only once a week she may play field hockey once a week.
• A neat appearance and good carriage [posture] are insisted on.

Today, both male and female fans pack the stands at women's college games. In fact, women's basketball is the most popular women's collegiate sport played in North America.

2 The Man Behind the Team

Coach Page was a quiet man. Neatly cropped, wavy hair topped off his tiny frame. He never raised his voice to his players. He rarely talked to them during games. When he did speak, he chose his words carefully.

Page taught only the basics of the game — nothing fancy or complicated. A sportswriter kidded, "The Grads are good, but those plays are so old they've got whiskers on them!"

Coach Page wasn't much of a joker. "If the girls are masters of a dozen plays," he said, "They can cope with any situation."

The Grads worked on their plays during two 90-minute practices a week. Before a big game they often practised during their lunch hour. Coach Page focused on ball handling, shooting, dribbling, and passing. But the most important skill was teamwork.

"Not only must every member of the team be an excellent player, but every member must work in harmony with every other member," said Page. "Teamwork was the secret to our success."

Players passed the ball up the court until one of them had a clear shot. This may not have been as exciting as one player rushing to the basket, but the quick passing and shooting wowed their fans.

Page expected his team to be dedicated. He told them, "You must play basketball, think basketball, and dream basketball."

Though players could date while at home, they were not allowed to go on dates during road trips. They could not smoke, and drinking alcohol was never allowed. They obeyed these rules because it was such an honour to be one of the Grads.

Above all, Page insisted that his players show sportsmanship. They were to play fair, and to win or lose with grace. During the 1920 provincial championship, this

Women Working Together

There was a time when people believed women could not play team sports. Teammates have to work together and think on their feet. People thought women were not up to the challenge. Instead, they were steered toward individual sports like golf, tennis, and archery.

sportsmanship was put to a test.

The Grads were up against the University of Alberta Varsity. The Grads played hard, using their simple but effective style. As always, they worked as a single unit. Together, they created a defence that was as solid as a wall. They won the game, but their victory was short-lived.

During the championship game, a Grads player was injured. McDougall Commercial High School student Connie Smith took her place. The Varsity said that Connie should not have been allowed to play because she was still a student. They thought only graduates should be allowed to play for the Grads. The Grads knew that playing the game again without Connie could mean losing, but they did not want to win unfairly. They did not fight the Varsity's protest and the game was replayed. As a result, the Grads lost the championship 30 to 22. It was their first big loss.

Seven months later, the Grads challenged the Varsity to a rematch. Both teams were confident they would win.

A Man Coaching Women?

Berenson had strong ideas about women's sports. One of them was that men do not make good coaches for female athletes. "They are only interested in developing a winning team," she said in a speech. "The hard grind of practice — not the joy of playing but to develop a winning team — the travelling of teams to different schools and towns, often unchaperoned, bring about nervous excitement, worry, sleeplessness, and all the evils of athletics." Was she right? Well, Coach Page did make his team practise hard. And they sure did win a lot of games! Since his players stayed on the team for years, perhaps it's fair to say that they disagreed with Berenson.

This time, it was no contest and there were no excuses. The Grads won easily — 25 to 3! They remained provincial champions for the next 20 years.

3 Making Their Mark

Sports are an important part of life for girls and women. In North America, they can play any sport they choose. The media celebrates the successes of female athletes. Girls can watch women's basketball pros and dream of following in their footsteps.

It wasn't always like this. People used to look down upon female athletes. They played with second-rate equipment and got little or no coaching. No one wanted to put money into promoting teams or sending them on tour. Imagine trying to train back then, when few people took women's sports seriously!

Not only did women have to compete against one another, they had to face off against public opinion. It was their greatest opponent.

The early Grads faced these barriers. Like other women, the players were told they shouldn't play games that were competitive and rough. They didn't listen. If men could play sports, why couldn't women?

When the team was formed, there was not much news coverage of women's sports. The papers hardly covered their many victories. Small blurbs were buried in the back of the sports pages. But the Grads kept winning. Over time, they began to seem unstoppable. Suddenly, local sportswriters took notice. Brief articles grew into long stories.

As the media coverage grew, so did the

crowds who came to the games. Young girls idolized the Grads. These fans began to dream about playing basketball, too. No one knew it then, but big changes were coming.

Women were excelling at sports around the globe. In the United Kingdom, nineteen-year-old swimmer Gertrude Ederle captured the world's attention with an amazing feat of endurance. This three-time Olympic gold medal winner became the first woman to swim across the English Channel. She even beat the previously set men's record.

She knew her accomplishment helped change public opinion about women in sport.

"People said women couldn't swim the Channel, but I proved they could," said Ederle.

The Grads didn't know the mark they would leave on the world. They just wanted to play basketball. As it turns out, this basketball team from Edmonton led the way to a golden age in women's sports.

4 Heading East

As older players retired from the team, Coach Page needed new athletes to replace them. The Grads were still connected to McDougall Commercial High School. They held all their practices in the gymnasium. Page was still a teacher there. He also coached the school's girls' basketball teams.

In fact, Page created a good training system through the high school. The girls started by playing on a junior team. This team was made up of students from grades 10 and 11. They then moved on to the senior team. Most of those players came from grade 12. However, strong athletes from lower grades sometimes made the lineup. Grade 12 students and graduates could also play for the Gradettes. This team was made up of players who were good enough to join the Grads, and who were waiting for an opening.

While the Grads always had players ready to join their lineup, only a few ever got the chance. Many players had long careers as Grads. Coach Page only carried eight or nine players on his roster. This left little room for new players. In total, just 38 women wore the Edmonton Grads' black-and-gold jerseys. That's not very many players, given the team's 25-year history!

Grads players were unmarried and had day jobs. Most were office employees, and some were teachers. The team took up almost all of their free time and energy. Becoming a wife meant taking on household duties. Only one player in the team's history could juggle married life and being a Grad.

With such dedicated players, the Grads kept getting stronger. The 1922 lineup was their best to date. It included six key players in the team's history.

Winnie Martin had been with the Grads since the team was created in 1915. She was the team's best all-around player. She could play both the forward and guard positions, and was a tough defender. Opponents rarely had a clear shot at the basket with Winnie around.

Connie Smith, now a graduate of McDougall Commercial High School, held down the other guard position. She was tall and used her height well on the court.

Eleanor Mountifield was the centre. She moved with grace. Newspapers praised her willowy figure and halo of golden hair. She was also a tough athlete at both ends of the court.

Forwards Nellie Perry and Daisy Johnson were known for their precise shooting. They raked up most of the points for the Grads. Teammates knew the surest way to score baskets was to get the ball into their hands.

At sixteen, Daisy's sister Dorothy

Edmonton Commercial Grads, first Dominion Champions, 1922

Johnson was the baby of the team. Although not very tall, she could jump higher than the average player could. She played alongside Eleanor at centre court.

In 1922, the Grads were the best in the West. At that time, there were no national basketball championships — for women's or for men's teams. However, sporting clubs in the East did not need a contest to decide who the best in the country was. Each year, the top eastern teams declared themselves the Canadian champs. The Grads decided they should have a chance to compete for that title. They issued a challenge to the 1922 eastern women's champions, the London Shamrocks.

The two-game playoff series would take place in the Shamrocks' hometown of London, Ontario. Whichever team scored the most points over the two games would be the Canadian champion.

It cost about $1,500 to send the Grads

east. The team had no money of its own. The London club put in $600. The Grads had to raise the rest. They agreed to play two exhibition games against teams in St. Thomas and Toronto, Ontario. Those teams were willing to pay the Grads for the chance to play them. These teams wanted to play the best in the West, knowing it would draw a crowd. Each player also chipped in $25 of her own money to help cover costs. Despite this, they could only afford to send six players: Winnie, Connie, Nellie, Eleanor, Daisy, and Dorothy. Of course, they didn't leave Coach Page behind!

The pride of Alberta was heading into new territory. They had no idea what was awaiting them.

5 New Territory

The buzz around the championship series grew quickly. All four of the Grads' matches were sold out before the team left Edmonton. In London, larger arenas were booked to make room for the crowds. "The quest of the local girls for the Canada title has attracted attention in all parts of the country," wrote the *Edmonton Journal*.

The journey east was over 3,000 kilometres (1860 miles). The Grads could not afford sleeper cars. They spent the three-day trip snoozing in their seats. Instead of eating in the dinner car, they ate packed meals. By the end of their journey, the players were tired and stiff. But it did not show on the court.

The *Journal* reported, "No sooner had the [first] game started than the Edmonton girls brought the thousand spectators to their feet."

Winnie and Connie gave the London forwards a lot of trouble. The Grads blocked shots and cut off passes. Centres Eleanor and Dorothy roamed midcourt. They had little trouble getting the ball to Nellie and Daisy, the team's forwards. The ball kept swishing into the net. Nellie even got a round of applause for a beautiful long running shot. By halftime, the Grads led the Shamrocks 32 to 4.

Basketball rules were different in the East. Eastern teams had five players on the

Five Instead of Six

Men's basketball in the West had similar rules to women's basketball in the East. Both played with five players on the court. To help train for matches against eastern teams, the Grads practised against local men's teams.

court. Westerners played with six. The Grads still followed the women's rules set down by Senda Berenson. It had been decided that the first game would follow western rules, and the second would follow eastern rules.

With only six players able to make the trip, the Grads had no rest during the first game. London tried to wear down the visitors. The Shamrocks called for seven time-outs to bring in fresh players of their own. This tactic did not work against the Edmonton team. Thanks to Coach Page's endless drilling practices, the Grads were in excellent shape. They won handily: 41 to 8.

The Shamrocks were fierce competitors. They had won two straight eastern championships. No team had ever beaten them. "It was a sad blow to local fans," wrote the *London Free Press*. "But the better team won."

The Grads headed off to St. Thomas for their exhibition game. This one was closer — 19 to 16 for Edmonton. The Grads went straight back to London for the second game of the championship series.

Following eastern rules meant one less player on the court. The rules also allowed for a rougher style of play. Coach Page knew it would be a battle. "I saw a men's game here last night," he wrote in a letter to the *Edmonton Journal*. "Everything goes, and I foresee a rough and tumble struggle in the finals."

He was right.

A record crowd of 1,500 showed up for the game. The *London Free Press* reported that it looked more like rugby than basketball! "Everything went," stated the newspaper. "Holding, blocking and tussling of every description. The spectators must have wondered how the [Grads] could hold up."

Time after time, the Grads fell to the floor. It is a wonder they were not seriously hurt. With five out of six team members on the court, only one player could rest at a time. The team was already tired from their train journey and the

Making Ends Meet

Exhibition games were played just for show. The games helped teams raise money and publicity. The results didn't count towards a season's totals.

exhibition game in St. Thomas. The halftime score was 12 to 2 — for the Shamrocks.

In the second half, the Grads stopped trying to score. Each player was assigned to a Shamrock. They stayed glued to their players, trying to keep them from making baskets. And the Grads toughened up. By the end of the game, London had taken only nine more points. Edmonton added six to their total.

The Shamrocks won the game, but it was not enough to take the title. The Grads won the series with a total of 49 points to the Shamrocks' 29. A 20-point spread! The Edmonton Grads became the first official Canadian women's basketball champions.

Before leaving Ontario, the new champs played an exhibition game against the Toronto All-Stars. The Grads won. Now they could return home and celebrate.

In those days, 80,000 people lived in Edmonton. Amazingly, 20,000 of them gathered to celebrate the Grads' return. A quarter of the city!

After stepping off the train, the Grads were hoisted onto the shoulders of their fans. They were carried through the crowd to waiting cars. The cars paraded from the train depot along the main drag, led by the Newsboys Band. As the Grads waved to their fans, children ran alongside them, cheering. Afterwards, they were honoured with banquets and gift presentations.

This was the Grads' first taste of widespread fame. The victory also thrust the city of Edmonton into the national spotlight. No other Edmonton team — in any sport, men's or women's — had ever won a Canadian championship.

The Grads put Edmonton on the sporting map.

6 Pride of Alberta

The Edmonton Grads did not find a lot of competition in Alberta. At the 1923 provincial championships, they played a team from Baron, Alberta. The team threw in the towel after the first half of the game because there was no hope of winning. The Grads took the title with a score of 22 to 2.

The secret to the Grads' success continued to be teamwork. Not only was each member a great player, they all worked well together. Players did not show off for the crowd, and no one was the star. They always behaved like a team.

The Grads' second series against the London Shamrocks is a great example of how the Edmonton squad clicked.

The Shamrocks had topped the eastern leagues. Once again, they would play the Grads with the Canadian championship at stake. The two-game series was played at the Edmonton Arena. It was really a hockey rink, but the Grads paid to put in a hardwood surface. Over 3,000 fans packed the stands. It was the biggest crowd in the history of Canadian basketball.

One advantage the Grads had was their size. They outweighed their eastern opponents! This made all the difference when the Grads were guarding their basket.

The Shamrocks' forwards tried to drive the ball into the Grads' end. The home guards watched them closely. Eleanor and rookie Mary Dunn were now the defensive duo. They clung to the London forwards "like a drowning man clutches at a straw," wrote the *Edmonton Journal*. They waited for the Shamrocks to pass. As the ball left their opponents' hands, they would steal it mid-air.

Dorothy and Winnie played the forward positions, with Connie at centre. They shot well, but they had to get the ball first. They relied on their teammates to make their famous quick passes. The Grads never hesitated. The passes flowed from player to player up the court.

Dorothy opened the Grads' scoring in the first game of the series. She took a cross-court pass, shooting from the far right corner. Swish! A few seconds later, Eleanor followed with another beautiful basket. Connie made the most dazzling shot of the game. She threw the ball from the centre of the court. It dropped through the hoop without even touching the edges.

The Grads defeated the Shamrocks, 17 to 6.

An even bigger crowd of 4,000 came to the second game. It was closer, but the Grads won again, 34 to 22. Dorothy was the Grads' top scorer with 14 points, followed by Connie's 10, and Winnie's 8.

Clearly, the best of the East was no match for the best of the West. But the Grads had been hearing things about another talented team. A women's basketball club in Cleveland, Ohio, was calling itself the world champion. They were the top team in the United States. Could the best of the South beat the best of the North?

The Grads issued a challenge. The Cleveland Favorite-Knits accepted it.

7 The Queens of the Court

The history of the Cleveland Favorite-Knits mirrored the Edmonton Grads' own history. The Knits had played together for many years. They learned the game as young girls at the Clark Avenue Gymnasium. The gym's manager, Julius Kemeny, became their coach. Their sponsor was Favorite-Knit Mills, a company that made sporting goods. It gave them money for things like uniforms and travel.

Like the Grads, the Knits were very loyal to their teammates. They refused offers to join other sports clubs in Cleveland or nearby cities, even when they were offered money to play. Teamwork was very important to these champs — and it paid off. By 1923, the Knits had been the top women's basketball team in the United States for four years. They had only lost four games in six years.

The Grads and the Knits would play a two-game, total-point series. The winner would be the official world champion. It was Edmonton's first world series in any sport. Now people were paying attention to women's basketball! "It is up to every booster in the city to get behind the Grads," wrote the *Edmonton Journal*. "Show them their efforts to put Edmonton on the map are appreciated."

The Knits asked the Grads for a fee of $2,000. That was too much for the

Edmonton team. Eventually they settled on $1,600.

The Grads prepared for the series by playing local men's teams. Playing bigger opponents took speed and skill. The women had plenty of both. It was also a chance to practise playing by the men's rules. Like the eastern teams in Canada, Cleveland followed the rules of men's basketball.

Tickets for the series sold quickly. People from towns across Alberta ordered them through the mail to ensure they didn't miss the matchup. Two sections of cheap seats were set aside for Edmonton children.

The Grads' lineup had not changed since the London series. On offence were forwards Winnie, Dorothy, and Connie. Guards Mary and Eleanor were again the Grads' defensive duo. Abbie Scott and Elizabeth Elrick joined Nellie as substitute players.

The Knits had many of their own stars. They included Eva Dachtler, Elizabeth Wagemaker, and Beatrice Schier, who played on the Knits' forward line. Guards Helen Fisher and Cathleen McAleer provided defence.

Before the first game, the Knits' captain, Elizabeth Wagemaker, spoke to the *Edmonton Journal*. "May the best team win," said Wagemaker. She added, "I hope that team is ours."

1923 Grads, winners of the Underwood International Trophy

Over 6,000 people jammed the Edmonton Arena to the rafters. The Canadian flag and the American flag hung side by side at the north end of the arena. Everyone stood at attention while the Newsboys Band played the American anthem "The Star-Spangled Banner," and the then-Canadian anthem "God Save the King."

The Knits wore shorts and jerseys bearing the bold words "World Champions." The Grads came out in their usual dress. They wore loose-fitting sailors' middies (blouses), pleated bloomers, and black-and-gold headbands. Based on their clothing, the Grads definitely looked like underdogs.

They were not. "The game hadn't been underway more than a minute or two when surprise … could be seen written large on the faces of Coach Kemeny and the Favorite-Knits," wrote the *Journal*.

The Knits tried a slow passing game. They wanted to draw the Grads away from their positions on the court. Once the Grads were far enough from the players they were supposed to be watching, the Knits would use a long pass to an open player. The player would then score an easy basket. That was the plan, anyway.

Cleveland's system failed. Coach Page had taught the Grads never to leave their positions. They were to cling to the opponent they were covering. "The Grads were on top of the players they were covering at every moment of the play," wrote the *Journal*. "It seemed impossible to get through (them)." Whenever the Knits tried a long pass, it was intercepted by the Grads.

Though they were playing well, the Grads still seemed to be on edge. "The big crowd seemed to worry the Grads more than the Knits," wrote the *Journal*.

"Dorothy Johnson was obviously nervous on her penalty throws early in the game."

The plays were read into a telephone and then broadcast by the Edmonton radio station CJCA. It reported that the Grads opened the scoring, but that the Knits quickly tied the game. The back and forth continued until Dorothy regained her nerve. She then became a scoring machine.

By the end of the first half, Dorothy scored 12 points. Every Grad on the starting lineup had also scored at least one point by halftime. The Grads took a 22 to 6 lead.

The Knits, however, pulled their game together in the second half. They started moving down the court at great speed. Wagemaker quickly scored five points. A basket by Fisher — a beautiful shot from the side of the hoop — brought the Knits within seven points. It was not enough.

Dorothy scored the final basket, her seventeenth point of the game. The final score was 34 to 20 for the Grads.

Going into the second game, local fans worried that the Knits "might have a few tricks 'up their sleeves'," wrote the *Journal*. If they did, the Grads never saw them. The Cleveland team once again relied on long passes. The Grads used short, snappy passes. They took many more shots on net than their opponents took.

Sports Sponsorships

Team sponsors give basketball clubs money to cover their costs. They help them buy uniforms, pay for court time, and travel to games. In the Knits' day, businesses across the United States sponsored sports teams. Many cities had leagues made of these sponsored teams. Cleveland was one of the leading cities in the United States in promoting amateur sport.

"Sweeping down the floor, the ball would change hands at least three times after the centre line had been crossed," wrote the *Journal*. "When the play was completed the one with the ball would only be a few feet away from the hoop."

When the final bell rang, the Grads were ahead 19 to 13. The total-points score for the series was 53 to 33, with the Grads on top. Once again, they took a major title with a 20-point lead.

The Grads were world champions! For

The Underwood Trophy

As world champions, the Grads were awarded a new trophy. The Underwood Typewriter Company donated a prize for the championship. The Underwood was a challenge trophy. Teams that won their league championship could challenge the Grads for the trophy.

the first time, the city of Edmonton was home to a world's-best sports team. The 7,000 fans in the arena jumped to their feet and cheered. From this point on, they would call their Grads "the queens of the court."

Both teams were in tears — of joy for one, of sadness for the other. They hugged and congratulated their opponents. "The Knits took their defeat with a smile," said the *Journal*.

Cleveland's captain Wagemaker waved merrily to the crowd. They answered back with a roar of approval. Before leaving the court, she told them, "You are wonderful. We hate to leave."

8 The Olympic Dream

The Edmonton Grads had three titles to defend in 1924. The first was the provincial championship. A series against the eastern champs for the Canadian title would follow. The Grads could then face teams challenging them for the world championship.

One day after practice, Coach Page asked the team to meet in the lobby of McDougall Commercial High School. Some players thought he was going to announce a challenge from another team. No one was prepared for what he was going to say.

In his usual calm voice, Page told his team that they had been asked to represent Canada at the next Olympics. The Games would take place in Paris, France. The players were stunned by what they heard. After a few seconds, their excitement overtook them.

A letdown followed Coach Page's good news, however. Soon afterwards, the Grads were told that they were not really competing at the Olympics. Basketball was not yet an official Olympic sport. The Grads would represent Canada in an international tournament. It would be held in Paris at the same time as the Olympics. The Grads would wear the Canadian colours: red and white.

Because they were not an Olympic team, the Canadian Olympic Committee would not cover their travel expenses. This presented a huge challenge for the Grads. They had to pay the entire cost of the trip to Europe — about $10,000.

The Grads would have to play for the money. Coach Page sent invitations to the top two women's teams in the United States. A larger playing surface was created at the Edmonton Arena. The floor size increased to 6,000 square feet (560 square metres) from 4,000 square feet (370 square metres). The court measured 100 feet by 60 feet (30 metres by 18 metres). It was the largest basketball court in Canada.

First, the Grads had to defend their provincial title. The two-game series against the University of Alberta Varsity took place in March. The Grads had yet to play a game that year. The Varsity hoped this would give them an edge over the world champions. But the Grads won both games of the series easily. It was their ninth provincial championship in 10 years.

In April, it was on to the Canadian championship. This time, the Toronto Maple Leafs had topped the eastern women's basketball league. The Grads took that two-game series as well. It was the twenty-fifth game in a row that they had won.

The world championships were scheduled for May 13. The Grads would face a new team: the Chicago Lakeviews. The Grads' supporters were worried. The American challengers had won 34 out of 35 league games that season. The Grads had played five games total.

Lack of competition back home could hurt the Grads' chances against the Lakeviews. Practices got players into physical shape, but games built toughness and teamwork. The Grads had not been tested that season.

"There are scores of fans who are shaking their heads," wrote the *Edmonton*

Journal. "The possibility of defeat [is] staring the Grads in the face."

Coach Page told the newspaper that he was not concerned. He was preparing his team by training hard three times a week.

Seven thousand Grads supporters filled the Edmonton Arena. Winnie and Mary were the Grads' starting guards. Connie at centre was flanked by forwards Dorothy and Daisy on the offensive line.

The Grads scored five points in the first few minutes. Then they lost their bearings, and the Lakeviews took four points. It looked as though the game would be a real battle. Then Connie looped a graceful shot through the hoop to make the score 7 to 4. By the end of the first period, the Grads were ahead 9 to 4.

In the second half, the Grads really hit their stride. They swept down the floor three abreast. With quick passes, they worked their way to the Lakeviews' basket.

The team from Chicago kept getting confused. They left their positions. Each time, a Grad jumped into the opening. Coach Page sent in Abbie to take Daisy's place. "Abbie was the last link in the Grads' chain [of players]," wrote the *Journal*. She scored 11 points.

The Grads did not always wait until a player had a clear shot at the basket. They began shooting from amazing distances. Abbie and Connie swished the ball into the net from the middle of the court, bringing the crowd to their feet.

At the end of the game, Connie was the top scorer with 13 points. The Grads defeated the Lakeviews, 44 to 11.

No one was more shocked than Chicago's coach, Hugh Wilson. After the game, he admitted that it was the "surprise of his life."

The Grads won the second game by another wide margin. The series totals were 86 to 21 for Edmonton. The city was still home to the Underwood trophy.

At one time, the Grads thought of themselves as giant killers: underdogs taking on bigger teams. Now they were the giant every team in the world wanted to topple.

The Federation Sportive Feminine International

The international women's basketball tournament was created by a special organization. The *Federation Sportive Feminine International* (FSFI) promoted women's sports in Europe. In 1922, they organized the first women's only Olympic-style tournament. 300 women from five countries competed at that first tournament. They would later arrange to hold their events at the same time as the Olympics.

9 Edmonton Versus the World

Many defeated teams wanted the chance to take on the Grads again. None wanted a rematch more than the Cleveland Favorite-Knits. They had been training hard for a year. Coach Kemeny assembled the best team he could. They were ready to challenge the Grads for their world championship title. They journeyed by train from Cleveland to Edmonton.

The Grads took all their games seriously, but this two-game set was extra important. It was their last competition before the international tournament. They did not know what the level of play was like on the other side of the Atlantic. This was their last chance to perfect their skills.

When the teams squared off in 1923, the Knits could not defeat the Grads' defensive style. The Knits had learned from this. Their playing style was now very similar to the Grads' style. What Cleveland didn't know was that Edmonton had also improved. Dorothy was no longer the team's chief scorer. Connie and Abbie were also sinking a lot of baskets.

"These two girls have come along like a house on fire," wrote the *Edmonton Journal*. "Coach Kemeny is due for the surprise of his life when he sees this pair (in action)."

When the Grads won the first match, Connie was the top scorer with eight points. In the second game, Connie went on a scoring rampage! Her shooting was brilliant: most of her 15 points were scored from across the court.

"The result was as good as settled before the first period was half over," reported the *Journal*.

The Grads won the series, 62 to 26 in total points. The final game was their twenty-ninth straight victory.

Now, the Grads looked toward becoming true world champions by winning the international tournament in Paris.

The Grads paid for the Chicago and Cleveland teams to play in Edmonton. Thankfully, Grads supporters filled the stands at all of their games. Ticket sales raised enough money for the team to go to Europe.

The Grads could send eight players and Coach Page. His wife came along as a chaperone to keep an eye on the women. The Grads' lineup included Winnie, Connie, Abbie, Mary, Dorothy, Nellie,

Eleanor, and Daisy. They would travel to the east coast by train. Then they would board an ocean liner for a nine-day trip across the Atlantic.

"Beat 'em Grads! Show 'em how it's done!" shouted the 2,000 fans who gathered at the Edmonton train depot. The eastbound train was delayed by the big send-off. The Newsboys Band played and the crowd cheered as the Grads boarded the train. The team waved to their hometown crowd until they were out of sight.

It took eight days to cross Canada by train. They were met by cheering fans at every stop. "No promises were made by the team. They would do the best they said and that was all," wrote the *Edmonton Journal*.

The Grads made a splash on the French basketball courts. Europeans had never seen basketball played with such precision. The Edmonton team's snappy passing and sharp shooting delighted the crowd, but puzzled their opponents. "All through the tournament the Grads played a brand of basketball that was a revelation to the onlookers," wrote the *Edmonton Journal*. The Grads' superior skills brought ovation after ovation.

The Grads' first important match was against a Parisian women's team. They played for the championship of France. In the first period, Parisian players carried the ball as far as Edmonton's basket. But the Grads did not allow a single shot on net.

The Canadians began scoring in the

A Dream Come True

Travelling to France was a dream come true for the Grads. Paris was a long way from the small city of Edmonton! The team visited places they had thought they would only ever see in pictures. The Eiffel Tower, for example, was a special treat for many players.

second period. They scored so often, the ball did not return to the defence area. In the final period, Paris managed to hold Edmonton to only six points. The Grads won the championship of France by a score of 67 to 17. Each member of the team proudly received a medal.

After the game, the Parisian team claimed that the team from Strasbourg, France, would defeat the Grads for the European title. Strasbourg had won four straight European championships. Were they any match for the Grads? Coach Page didn't think so. He believed the European teams did not have the right system to stand up to the Grads.

He was right, as usual. The Canadians defeated the Strasbourg squad, 37 to 8. The Grads went on to beat four more European teams. They were now on top of the world.

10 Heading into Disaster

The international tournament marked the end of the playing careers of several Grads. Winnie had been on the team for 10 years. Veterans Nellie, Abbie, and Eleanor also retired from the team.

Coach Page was never without enough talent, however. There were always players from the Gradettes ready to fill empty positions. In 1925, Elsie Bennie, Hattie Hopkins, and Kate MacKrae joined the Grads' lineup. Instead of having five starters and three subs, he had five starters and two subs.

The rookies enjoyed a glorious first year. The Grads went on a four-city western tour. They defended their Canadian championship and hung onto the Underwood trophy through four separate challenge series. The Grads did not lose a game all season.

The 1926 basketball season presented a new challenge for the Grads. They had played host to teams from cities across North America. Now it was their turn to hit the road. They prepared to invade basketball courts across the eastern United States and Canada.

J. Alex Sloan was a well-known sports promoter in the United States. He signed the Grads to a tour. Sloan billed the team as the "Pride of Edmonton." They would play the champions from different state and city leagues. The schedule was unknown when the team first signed on for the tour. However, the Grads knew they would be defending their Canadian and world championship titles. The Grads learned they would play 10 games. They would board an eastbound train on April 1 and return home on April 19. Playing 10 games in 12 days would put their stamina to the test!

The Grads kicked off the tour with wins in Winnipeg, Chicago, and Warren, Ohio. But the next series would haunt the Grads.

On April 8, 9, and 10, they were up against the Cleveland Newman-Sterns. Many of the Cleveland players were familiar to the Grads. They were all former Cleveland Favorite-Knits players, including Knits captain Elizabeth Wagemaker.

It was a four-game series. Whichever team had the most total points would win the series. The Cleveland players had lost the world championship to Edmonton when they played for the Knits in 1923. This was a chance to take it back. Ten thousand Cleveland fans came out to support them.

The Newman–Sterns played at a high speed. The Grads appeared drawn and overworked. Their passing plays were gummed up, time after time. Nothing went right. Cleveland won the opening match.

"Everybody in attendance knew the better team won. The Grads knew it too," wrote the *Edmonton Journal*.

The Grads reversed their fortunes the following night. Connie really turned it on. Cries were heard all over the arena: "Watch Connie Smith!" She was a sharp shooter all night, making eight baskets. The Johnson sisters passed the ball well, creating many scoring chances. They also scored seven points each. Kate and Elsie — both in their second season for the Grads

— blocked many Cleveland plays. The final score was 26 to 21, for the Grads.

The last two games of the series were played in New York City. The Grads once again showed signs of fatigue. By contrast, the Newman-Sterns were still in top shape. They won the third game, and took a 59 to 52 total-point lead going into the final game.

The Grads had played strong teams before. But six games in as many nights wore them out. Down by seven points, they still had a chance to win the series. Did they have it in them?

The Grads were tired, and they were playing with another disadvantage. The courts in Cleveland and New York both had plate-glass backboards behind the baskets. Bouncing a ball off a clear backboard is very different from hitting a white wooden board. The Grads couldn't judge the distance to the basket. They missed many easy baskets in the third game. Even Connie and Dorothy seemed to be struggling.

The day of the final game, the Grads woke up ready to do battle. "Every girl on the team told me this morning that she is prepared to fight to the last ditch," wrote sports reporter George Macintosh for the *Edmonton Journal*.

It was not enough. The Clevelanders were in top form, while Edmonton still lacked their usual snap. The Grads' flashy passing did not outwit the Newman-Sterns. Cleveland took the final game of the series. The score was 13 to 8. It was the lowest score in the Grads' history. Even worse, the Clevelanders won the total-point series, 72 to 60. The Newman-Sterns were the new world champions.

After a day of rest, the Grads went to Toronto to defend the Canadian championship. Their opponents were the

Toronto Lakesides. This was a chance to save face after the shocking loss of their world title.

"When champions fall they fall with a resounding thud," wrote the *Edmonton Journal*. The weary Grads lost the first of the two-game series against the Lakesides.

Before the championship final, the Grads had a small boost. They played an exhibition game against a London squad and won 40 to 15.

The Lakesides started the deciding game with a five-point lead. The Grads did not allow their rivals many chances to shoot near the basket. Edmonton, on the other hand, was an offensive machine, finding the basket at all angles. Connie was a firecracker, scoring 15 points.

"Connie lived up to all the good things said of her before the team played in the east," wrote the *Edmonton Journal*. "[She] convinced the sportswriters of Toronto that she has class written all over her."

The Johnson sisters also did their part. Daisy took six points and Dorothy took four. The Grads' three top scorers showed off their terrific passing plays. "It was so good it had most of the fans up on their feet yelling and most of them were Toronto rooters," said the *Journal*.

The Grads won the second game, 27 to 6. And they held onto their Canadian championship by winning the total-point series, 46 to 30. It was a huge relief.

Back in Edmonton, many believed the Grads would soon have a chance to challenge again for the world championship title. But the Newman–Sterns ended their playing season after their victory against the Grads. Edmonton tried to press Cleveland into a series. But they would have to wait until the next year.

The Grads did not disappoint their hometown. In 1927, they beat the

Newman-Sterns in a two-game series. The Underwood trophy was theirs again. But losing it the previous year would not be their last defeat.

11 Old Opinions Die Hard

Even with all the positive changes in women's sports, there was still a long way to go. People still made it hard for women by not allowing them into the Olympics. Women were not yet welcome on the international sporting stage.

In the Grads' time, Olympic organizers did not want any women's sports in the Games. In particular, Baron Pierre de Coubertin, the man who started the modern Games in 1896, held this opinion.

And he wasn't afraid to make himself heard! "Their primary role should be like in the ancient tournament," Coubertin said. He declared that women should just help with "the crowning of the (male) victors with laurels." In other words, he thought women should hand out medals, not wear them.

The FSFI fought for women's rights in sports. They continued to arrange their own North American and European tournaments, but never stopped trying to get women into the "real" Olympics.

Finally, in 1924, women were allowed to compete in a handful of events at the Games. The sports included swimming, golf, tennis, fencing, sailing, and archery. It was the same year that the Grads won the FSFI tournament in Paris.

In protest, Coubertin quit as head of the International Olympic Committee. He didn't want to be part of an Olympics that included women.

Women's track and field events were added to the Amsterdam Olympics in 1928. Women competed in five track and field events, compared to the men's 22. Still, it was a huge step forward for female athletes.

The Canadian Olympic Committee decided to send a small team of women to Amsterdam to compete in the track and field events. These six athletes became known as the Matchless Six. They were Fanny "Bobbie" Rosenfeld, Ethel Smith, Jean Thompson, Myrtle Cook, Ethel Catherwood, and Jane Bell. They brought home four medals: two gold, one silver, and one bronze. Catherwood's gold medal remains the only individual gold medal ever won by a Canadian woman in track and field.

The Canadian women's team was also the overall winner in the women's track and field championship. They were celebrated as heroes back in Canada.

Sadly, these changes at the Olympics didn't extend to the basketball court. Once again, the FSFI held a tournament at the same time. And once again the Grads won every game they played.

Grads, Margaret McBurney and Gladys Fry, with J. Percy Page, 1931

From Runner to Writer

Fanny "Bobbie" Rosenfeld of the Matchless Six is one of Canada's most famous athletes. In 1950, sportswriters voted her Canada's Female Athlete of the Half Century, 1900 to 1950. She was also among the first people to be inducted into Canada's Sports Hall of Fame.

Rosenfeld is best known for her success at track and field events. At the 1928 Olympics in Amsterdam, she won gold in the 4 x 100 metre relay and silver in the 100 metre sprint. But Rosenfeld wasn't just a star runner. She excelled at hockey, baseball, tennis, and basketball. She played for two eastern basketball teams. Both teams challenged the Edmonton Grads for the Canadian championship in 1925 and 1928. The Grads won both series.

In 1933, Rosenfeld's career was cut short due to severe arthritis. Pain in her joints kept her bedridden for months. She needed a cane to help her walk for the rest of her life. That didn't slow her down, though!

By the 1930s, women's sports were very popular across Canada. Newspapers were finally giving female athletes the space they deserved. They hired former athletes to cover the women's sport scene. Among them were Rosenfeld and fellow Matchless Six member Myrtle Cook. Rosenfeld wrote for the *Globe and Mail* and Cook for the *Montreal Star*. They were the only female sports reporters at those newspapers.

In Edmonton, another famous name was writing for the sports pages. Coach Page's daughter, Patricia Page, wrote a column for the *Edmonton Journal* called "Feminine Flashes."

The Grads hoped women's basketball would finally become an Olympic event at the 1932 Games in Los Angeles, California. The sport was becoming more popular around the world. Crowds flocked to see their games. But it was not to be.

The Grads refused to play in the 1932 international women's tournament. If they could not play in the real Olympics, they did not want to play at all. A letter from the team was printed in the *Edmonton Journal*. It said: "The Grads will not take part in this year's Olympics for the simple reason that basketball is not included in the list ' of official or demonstration games."

In the end, the Grads went to Los Angeles, but they mostly sat on the sidelines and watched the games. While travelling to Los Angeles, they played three exhibition matches. They wanted to show people what they were missing. The games took place in San Francisco, Victoria, and Prince Rupert. Though they won the games, they returned home bitterly disappointed.

12 Cross-border Battle

At the 1932 Olympics in Los Angeles, the FSFI announced it would include basketball on the program at the women-only Olympic-style event being held in London in 1934. It was another chance for the Grads to prove themselves on the international stage.

In 1933, a new women's basketball championship was created. It was a best-in-five series between the national champs of the United States and Canada. The winner would represent North America at the women's Olympic-style tournament.

The Grads were up against the Durant Cardinals. The Cardinals played for the Durant Presbyterian Ladies College in Oklahoma. A trip to Europe was on the line.

Winnie Martin, Connie Smith, Mary Dunn, and Dorothy Johnson were names of the past. Now it was up to players such as Margaret MacBurney, Gladys Fry, Elsie Bennie, Babe Belanger, and Doris Neale.

The series was played in Edmonton. A few minutes into the first game, the Grads made four two-point baskets. With an 8 to 0 lead, the crowd at the Edmonton Arena sat back. It seemed certain their team would win.

But the Durant squad did not travel all that way to lose. They blasted onto the scoreboard. By the end of the first quarter, the Grads' lead was just 10 to 8.

The Cardinals were a talented team.

They were in better shape than any other opponent the Grads had faced. They were

Coach Page and Grads captain, Etta Dann

tall and they rarely missed a basket. The Cardinals also played solid offence and defence. By the third quarter, things were not looking good for Edmonton. The fans were in an uproar. Then the final whistle blew. There was a hush.

The crowd rose. The winning team was owed their applause. The Cardinals had beaten the Grads, 59 to 52.

It got worse. After three games, the Cardinals were ahead. The Grads had never lost more than a single game on their home court. Now they had lost three in a row.

The fourth game had a "killing pace," reported the *Edmonton Journal*. The Grads took a five-point lead early in the game. It melted away. Every time the Grads gained a lead, the Cardinals took it away. Both teams were worn out by the battle.

In the end, the Grads were "outweighed and outdistanced by the tall girls from the

Ozark hills," said the *Journal*. The Cardinals won again. They went on to take the North American title.

The loss caused "a genuine sadness in practically every home in Edmonton and district," wrote the *Journal*.

No one could have been sadder than the Grads and their coach. They had lost in front of their city. And they would not be playing at the Olympic-style tournament.

Fighting for Equality

The 1934 FSFI women's Olympic-style tournament would be their last. The addition of women's events at the Olympics meant there was less need for a women-only event. The organization only lasted 12 years, but it played an important role in bringing equality to sport.

13 Shooting Star

Their loss to the Cardinals shook the
Grads. Like many of the teams they had
defeated, the Grads wanted a rematch.
They did not get a chance until 1936.

That year, the Cardinals got a new
sponsor — an Arkansas oil company. They
were moved to El Dorado, Arkansas, and
were renamed the El Dorado Lions. The
Lions challenged the Grads for the
Underwood trophy.

The American team had an impressive

record. They had won 91 straight games. They were also made up of the same tall players that defeated the Grads in the series on their home court. To prepare, the Grads played against the tallest players from McDougall Commercial High School's boys' basketball team.

The three-out-of-five game series would be the last for many Grads. Afterwards, Babe, Gladys, and Doris hung up their jerseys. It was also the first series for new talent, such as Mabel Munton, Helen Northrup, Etta Dann, and Sophia Brown.

One of the team's best players was Noel MacDonald. She had been playing for the Grads since 1933. She was a rookie when the Grads lost to the Cardinals. Now she was a top scorer. Could she get the ball past the tall Lions?

More than 4,000 people wedged into the Edmonton Arena for the first game. Thousands more listened to the radio for the play-by-play. It must have sounded familiar. The Grads took an early lead — as they did in games against the Cardinals. And as before, they could not keep it.

Fans believed "the home talent would dish up one of their famous rallies before the finish and end up on the right side," wrote the *Journal*.

No such luck.

The Grads narrowed the Lions' lead to a single point, 33 to 32. But it was the visitors who had the winning rally. Edmonton lost 44 to 40.

In the second match, the Grads had more fighting spirit. Noel showed why she was the team's rising star. She scored eight points and edged the Grads in front. The score traded back and forth between the teams.

With less than 30 seconds left in the game, the Grads were two points behind. No one "would have given a plugged nickel for their winning chances," stated the *Journal*.

But Noel was not finished. She sunk a basket and evened the score, 35 to 35. The crowd's roar rattled the rafters. When play resumed, the Grads moved with lightning speed. Noel once again had the ball. She was within shooting range of the Lions' basket. The ball soared through the air. It swished through the net's strings just as the timer's gun went off.

"It couldn't have been timed more

The Grads in Europe, 1936

exactly if it had been rehearsed over a hundred times," wrote the *Journal*.

Victory for the Grads!

Fans tossed their hats into the air. They climbed over seats and swarmed the floor. Noel was carried on their shoulders. Babe cried grateful tears onto Elsie's shoulder.

The next two games were no less exciting. The Grads took the third and fourth games to win three of five. The Underwood trophy would stay Edmonton.

More than 12,000 tickets were sold for the series against the Lions. The ticket sales helped pay for the Grads' next journey across the Atlantic.

The Grads were invited to compete at an international tournament that would be held at the same time as the 1936 Olympics in Berlin, Germany. Women's basketball was not yet an official Olympic sport. The Grads would have to pay their own way to Europe.

Previously, the Canadian Olympic Committee had done nothing for the Grads as they fought for their sport to be included in the Games. This changed in 1936.

The committee gave the Grads an unusual compliment. They cabled Germany and asked if the Grads could march in the opening parade of athletes at the Olympics. The German organizers agreed. The Grads became part of the

The Olympic team in Strasbourg, 1936

Canadian delegation.

Eight Grads travelled to Berlin along with Coach Page. They wore the Canadian colours, red and white, in the nine-game series. They won all nine games.

Tragedy ended the Grads' Olympic dream for good. The 1936 Olympics had been hosted by German leader Adolph Hitler. Three years later, Canada was fighting with England against Germany in the Second World War. With the world in chaos, the 1940 Olympics were cancelled. The team would not last to see another Olympics.

Forty Years of Waiting

In 1936, men's basketball became an official Olympic event. Female players had to wait another 40 years! Women's basketball finally became an official Olympic sport at the 1976 Games in Montreal, Quebec.

14 End of an Era

Between 1937 and 1939, the Grads lost only one game. One of their players also received a great honour. In fact, it was the greatest individual honour in Canadian sport. Noel was named the winner of the 1938 Lou Marsh award as Canada's top athlete.

Even so, the Grads were having a tough time. By 1940, it was hard to find Canadian teams willing to take them on. Then, the Amateur Athletic Union of

America (AAU) barred their women's basketball teams from playing in Canada.

Canadian women's teams now played by the same rules as the American men's teams. The American women's teams followed different rules. The AAU decided that it was unfair for their women's teams to have to switch rules when they travelled north.

The decision rocked the basketball world. Many American women's teams did not mind playing by the men's rules. They wanted to challenge the Grads for the Underwood trophy. They did not get their chance. The decision meant the Underwood trophy championship was no more.

The Grads faced other problems. With no strong opponents, their games were not as exciting. Fewer fans came to cheer them on. They played less often and made less money. This also made it hard to fund McDougall Commercial High School teams.

Coach Page had become the principal

of the school. He had new duties taking up his time.

Things went from bad to worse. The Grads could go no further. They were at the top of their sport, but no one would or could play them. They did not even have a home. Canada was fighting in the Second World War in Europe. The Canadian Air Force needed the Edmonton Arena, the Grads' home, for training.

On April 11, 1940, the team made a statement. They would stop playing as of June 6. The school teams would also be finished.

An amazing career deserved an amazing ending. The Grads hosted exhibition series against the Wichita Thurstons and Chicago's Queen Anne Aces. These U.S. teams were not part of the organizing body that stopped other Americans from playing in Canada. Could they be the last opponents to topple the Grads?

The last Grads lineup had a mixture of veterans and rookies. Among those who had been playing for the Grads for years were Helen, Mabel, Etta, and Sophia. Jean Williamson and younger players Kay MacRitchie and Betty Bawden were also part of the final team.

The Grads showed their usual flash in the series against the Thurstons. They won all three games easily. Sadly, only a few hundred people showed up for the series. The Grads were shocked and hurt. Edmonton was famous for supporting their team.

Their fans did not let them down during the final series, however. They filled the arena to watch the Grads take on the Queen Anne Aces.

"The old gang was all here," wrote the *Edmonton Journal*.

Thirty-six former Grads were in the crowd. They watched their team win the first game 56 to 34.

The second victory was narrower: 45 to 38.

There was just one game left. A Grads reunion was planned for June 6. Every player who ever wore a Grads' uniform was expected to be there.

"Tomorrow night, Edmonton Grads will be no more than a memory," wrote the *Edmonton Journal*. "But they'll be a memory that will last a long time with thousands of Edmontonians."

The year 1940 was not only the Grads' last. It was also their twenty-fifth anniversary. It was a time to celebrate their beginning and mourn their ending.

They had been called "the queens of the court." They were champions in Edmonton, Alberta, Canada, and the world. They had travelled more than 140,000 kilometres (over 86,900 miles) chasing victory. Dr. Naismith was one of the Grads' biggest fans. He said they were "the finest team that ever stepped out onto a basketball floor."

Over 6,000 fans came to pay tribute to their team at the final game. The Grads gave them one last victory. They defeated the Queen Anne Aces, 62 to 52.

"There is no other team in the world today that could successfully challenge the claims of the Grads," wrote the *Edmonton Journal*. "They are tops. And they are through."

Coach Page said, simply, "All good things have to come to an end."

The *Journal* added: "Come next fall and next spring, a lot of folks are going to miss their basketball games. You won't see their like again."

The All-Time All-Stars

After the final game, sports journalists named the top 10 Grads of all-time. Those players would become known as the "All-Time All-Stars." The Grads held a contest. Fans who chose all the names on the final list, in the correct order, would win a prize. Seventeen guessers got it right and shared the $500 prize. The top 10 rankings for the Grads' All-Time, All-Star team were:

- Noel MacDonald
- Etta Dann
- Margaret MacBurney
- Gladys Fry
- Babe Belanger
- Mabel Munton
- Elsie Bennie
- Helen Northrup
- Millie McCormack
- Connie Smith

Epilogue

When the Grads retired, the Underwood trophy retired with them. They were presented with the prize that they had held for almost seventeen straight years.

Coach Page's former players scattered in many different directions. Some remained in Alberta, while others moved halfway around the globe. But they were forever Edmonton Grads. They held reunions every six years and remained friends throughout their lives.

In 1974, the Grads were inducted into the Alberta Sports Hall of Fame. Though the Grads were known for their teamwork, one player was singled out for her special talent. Noel MacDonald, who had been named Canada's top athlete in 1938, was inducted into the Canadian Sports Hall of Fame in 1971.

As for their coach, J. Percy Page was inducted into the Alberta Sports Hall of Fame, the Canadian Sports Hall of Fame, and the Naismith Memorial Basketball Hall of Fame in Springfield, Massachusetts. He went on to become a politician. In 1940, he was voted into the provincial government and later he became Alberta's Lieutenant Governor.

In total, the Grads played 522 games. They won 502 and lost just 20. It was — and still is — a record that has never been beaten by any team in any sport.

Just as importantly, the Commercial

Graduates Basketball Club of Edmonton helped change beliefs about women in sport. They opened many doors for female athletes. The girls' team that got their coach through a coin toss loss set the standard for competitive women's basketball.

Glossary

Assist: A pass that leads to a field goal

Basketball court: A rectangular playing surface that has baskets at either end

Bounce pass: A throw that strikes the floor before it reaches the receiver

Centre: A player who is responsible for defending the basket and rebounding

Chest pass: A two-handed throw that moves from the passer's chest in a straight line to the chest area of the receiver

Defence: The team not holding the ball; a specific pattern of play used by a defending team

Dribbling: Bouncing the ball continuously

Field goal: A basket scored on any shot other than a free throw

Foul: A violation resulting from illegal contact with an opposing player

Forward: A player who is responsible for scoring and rebounding

Free throw: An unguarded shot taken from behind the free-throw line after a foul

Guard: A player who is usually responsible for setting up offensive plays

Jump shot: A throw made while jumping

Layup: A shot taken close to the basket that is usually banked off the backboard towards the basket

Offence: The team that has the ball; a pattern of play that a team uses while attempting to score

Pass: An intentional throw to a teammate

Rally: To get new energy and pull ahead to win a match

Starting lineup: A group of five players — two guards, one centre, and two forwards — who begin a game; also known as the 2-1-2 lineup

About the Author

RICHARD BRIGNALL is a journalist from Kenora, Ontario, who has written for such publications as *Cottage Life* and *Outdoor Canada*. He was previously the sports reporter for the *Kenora Daily Miner and News*. He co-authored, with John Danakas, the Recordbooks volume *Small Town Glory*.

Photo Credits

We gratefully acknowledge the Provincial Archives of Alberta for permission to reproduce the images within this book and on the cover.